Bible For Boys: Bible Story Picture Book For Kids

Speedy Publishing LLC
40 E. Main St. #1156
Newark, DE 19711

www.speedypublishing.com

Noah's Ark

Noah was a man who loved God dearly and worships God with all his heart.
Although everyone around him laughed and mocked Noah for believing in God. One day, God talked to Noah and told him that he will punish all that the wicked and only Noah's family will be saved from his wrath.

Noah went to his people and warned everyone about the great flood. But instead, they mocked and laughed at him as usual. So Noah went to his family and they started to build the ark. He followed every instructions God gave to Noah.

Everyone around Noah and his family was laughing at Noah for building such ark. He kept telling everybody they should believe in God so that they will be saved, but no one listened.

Soon, Noah got everything ready. He gathered enough supplies that will last for a long time. And Noah was also told by God to gather animals, two of each species. From the smallest to the largest animals, Noah and his family marched the animals into the ark.

People laughed and laughed at Noah and his family, still, they never believed in God.

Finally, all the animals were aboard. Noah, his wife, his three sons, and their wives entered the ark and shut it.

Then the great rain came. Thunders clashed and the rain never stopped for forty days and forty nights. The earth was flooded by the enormous downpour. The people outside were asking for help, but it was too late for them.

Floodwaters destroyed the towns and the villages. The mountains underwent the great flood and rain until everything became quiet and still.

As the ark floated on the floodwater, Noah and his family along with animals were safe inside the ark.

For five months, there was flood. But God sent a dry wind over the ark. Noah and his family stayed inside the ark waiting for God to take them on safety waters.

Noah went outside to send out a raven and a dove. The raven never came back, but the dove went home. A week later, Noah tried to send out the dove again but this time the dove went back with a new olive leaf in its beak. Another week later, Noah sent out the dove but the dove did not return.

Noah then told his family that they are now safe to disembark from the ark. God also told Noah that it is time to go out.

Off they went along with the animals and Noah and his family praised God for protecting and saving them from the great flood.

David and Goliath

It was a long, long time ago, King Saul was the king of Israel, and there was a young boy named David. David had seven brothers and they look after their father's flock. David was the youngest and yet he was the bravest and he has a strong faith in God. He lived in the town called Bethlehem.

With the help of David's strong faith to God, he was protected by God in all kinds of dangers. Meanwhile, the prophet of God, Samuel was sad because King Saul disobeyed God. God then told Samuel to go over David's father, Jesse.

Samuel went to Jesse, as God commanded, which made King Saul very angry. When Samuel saw David, he told David that he was the anointed one by the Lord.

Back into Saul's kingdom, Saul became a troubled man. So his servants seek for someone who can play the harp well, and that was David. David soothed Saul and helped him to regain his senses. When David went home, the Philistines attacked the kingdom of Saul. David's brothers went to fight for Saul's army. David was then sent by his father, Jesse, to see how his brothers are doing.

During the battle there was a huge and gigantic Philistine warrior named Goliath. Every Israelite soldier is scared of Goliath. Goliath challenged everyone to kill him, and if someone is able to kill him, they will become servants to Israelites. But, if Goliath is not killed then the Israelites will become their servants. Sadly, all the men fled and did not dared fighting against Goliath.

Then David told Saul that he will fight this Philistine. David did not wear any armor but only took his sling and five smooth stones. Goliath laughed when he learned that a young boy is going against him. But David said, "I came to you in the name of the Lord. This day He will deliver you into my hands, for the battle is the Lord's." David then ran towards Goliath and fired the slingshot. The stone went right straight to Goliath's head and stroked him down.

Adam and Eve

The LORD God took the man and put him in the Garden of
Eden to work it and take care of it. And the
LORD God commanded the man, "You are free to eat from any
tree in the garden ;
but you must not eat from the tree of the knowledge of good
and evil, for when you eat of it you
will surely die."
Genesis 2:15-17

Now the serpent was more crafty than any of the wild animals
the LORD God had made. He said to the woman , "Did God
really say, 'You must not eat from any tree in the garden'?" The
woman said to
the serpent, "We may eat fruit from the trees in the garden, but
God did say, 'You must not eat fruit from the tree that is in the
middle of the garden, and you must not touch it, or you will die.'
"You will not surely die ," the serpent said to the woman. "For
God knows that when you eat of it your eyes will be opened, and
you will be like God, knowing good and evil."
Genesis 3:1-5

When the woman saw that the fruit of the tree was good for
food and pleasing to the eye, and also desirable for gaining
wisdom, she took some and ate it. She also gave some to her
husband,
who was with her, and he ate it. Then the eyes of both of them
were opened , and they realized they were naked; so they sewed
fig leaves together and made coverings for themselves.
Genesis 3:6-7

Then the man and his wife heard the sound of the LORD God as he was walking in the garden in the cool of the day, and they hid from the LORD God among the trees of the garden. But the LORD God called to the man, "Where are you?" He answered , "I heard you in the garden, and I was afraid because I was naked; so I hid." And he said, "Who told you that you were naked? Have you eaten from the tree that I commanded you not to eat from?" The man said, "The woman you put here with me-she gave me some fruit from the tree , and I ate it." Then the LORD God said to the woman , "What is this you have done?" The woman said, "The serpent deceived me, and I ate." Genesis 3:8-13

The LORD God made garments of skin for Adam and his wife
and clothed them. And the LORD God said, "The man has now
become like one of us, knowing good and evil. He must not be
allowed to reach out his hand and take also from the tree of life
and eat, and live forever." So the LORD God banished him from
the Garden of Eden to work the ground from which he had been
taken. After he drove the man out, he placed on the east side of
the Garden of Eden a cherubim and a flaming sword flashing
back and forth to guard the way to the tree of life.
Genesis 3:21-24

So the LORD God said to the serpent , "Because you have done this , "Cursed are you above all the livestock and all the wild animals!
You will crawl on your belly and you will eat dust all the days of your life.

And I will put enmity between you and the woman , and between your offspring and hers; he will crush your head, and you will strike his heel."
Genesis 3:14-15

Story of Moses

A new king who was called Pharaoh came into power in Egypt. He didn't like it that there were so many Israelites and he thought they would one day take over the land. So he decided to make all the Israelites into slaves. He made them work from early in the morning till late at night doing very hard work. Even if they were tired the Egyptians wouldn't give them a break, they would just make them work harder. It was very bad.

Pharaoh did all this and he still wasn't happy. The Israelites were still growing in number so he decided to make a law. If any boys were born to the Israelites he would have them killed.

At this time there was an Israelite couple who were expecting to have a baby. When they had a baby boy (whose name would later be Moses) they decided to hide him because they wouldn't let anyone kill this beautiful, precious baby of theirs.

They hid Moses for three months, but as he got older he didn't sleep as much and he cried louder than before. So his parents did the only thing they could do, they made a strong basket (sort of like a mini baby boat) and put blankets around the baby and placed the basket in some tall grass in the Nile river.

Baby Moses had a sister named Miriam, and she watched from a distance to see what would happen to her baby brother. While she was watching she saw somebody coming, she realized it was Pharaoh's daughter and her servants. They were dressed like they were famous, and she had seen her before and remembered what she looked like.

Pharaoh's daughter had come for a swim. While she was swimming she noticed a basket floating a little ways away in the tall grass. So she asked one of her servants to go see what it was.

The girl brought the basket over to her, and when Pharaoh's daughter opened it, the light startled Moses so he woke up and started to cry. "What a sweet, beautiful little baby. It must be one of the Israelite's," Pharaoh's daughter said to her servants.

Miriam had seen what had happened, and she hurried over and asked, "Would you like me to go find an Israelite woman to feed the baby for you?"

"Yes, go and find someone who can nurse the baby." she answered. Miriam ran as fast as she could and told her mother that Pharaoh's daughter had found him and wanted someone to come nurse him.

They went and found Moses with Pharaoh's daughter, and she asked them, "Please help me and nurse this baby, and I will pay you for helping me."

Later he became the son to Pharaoh's daughter, and that's when she named him Moses, which means she got him out of the water.

After Moses had grown up, and was probably a little older than your parents, he was getting fed up with how his people were treated by Pharaoh. They still had to work so hard all these years later.

One day Moses saw an Egyptian beating a Hebrew, one of his own people, and he became so upset that he killed the Egyptian. After that Moses had to run away from Egypt because the Pharaoh found out what he'd done and was very angry with Moses.

Moses ended up in a place called Midian. He had stopped to rest by a well when seven sisters came by to give their father's sheep some water. In the middle of feeding the sheep some shepherds came by and started to become very rude.

They pushed the women aside and told them to get out of the way, that they needed the water more than they did. Moses saw all this and said to the shepherds, "These women were here first and they need the water just as badly as you do. If you have a problem take it up with me, but leave them alone and wait your turn."

The shepherds listened to Moses, and Moses stayed and helped feed the sheep for the sisters. When the sisters got home their father asked them, "How did you get done so early today?" They answered, "An Egyptian rescued us from some shepherds, and he even drew the water out of the well for us and watered the whole flock."

"Please, go and get him and invite him for supper," the father said. When they found Moses, and had talked with him for a while, they realized he had no place to stay. He ended up staying with them, and later married one of the sisters whose name was Zipporah. Moses became a shepherd, and took care of many animals. As the years went by the Pharaoh in Egypt died, but the Hebrews were still slaves and they prayed to God for help. God heard them and felt bad for them, He knew just what He was going to do next...

Now Moses was out looking after some sheep and after a while ended up near a hill. He was just talking to the sheep, like he always did when there was no one else to talk to, when he noticed a bush on fire. Moses sat and watched it for a while because something wasn't right. The bush was completely on fire, but it wasn't burning up the bush; there was no smoke, just fire. Moses decided to get closer and take a better look. As he approached the bush a voice came from the inside of it, "Moses! Moses!" Moses thought that this might be God, after all who else could speak from a bush that was on fire, but wasn't burning.

Moses replied, "I am here." He continued to walk closer to the bush but as he got closer God said to him, "Don't come any closer, take off your sandals because you are in the presence of God. I am the God of your father, the God of Abraham, the God of Isaac, and the God of Jacob."

These were men that Moses had heard about. He knew that God had done great things for these men, and He believed in their God. So when Moses heard God say these words he was afraid and covered his face with his cloak. He thought that if he saw God's face he would die because God is so bright and powerful.

Then God said to Moses, "I have seen all the pain my people have had to go through in Egypt. I have heard their prayers and want to save them from their slavery. I want to take them to another place where there is lots of good land and plenty of milk and honey. So Moses, I am sending you to free the Israelites from Pharaoh."

"Um, pardon me God but I think your talking to the wrong person. This is just me Moses I'm just a regular guy, Pharaoh won't listen to me," Moses said in disbelief. And God said, "I will be with you and will help you. So go to the Israelites and tell them I have sent you and I have heard their prayers, and will send them to a better place. Don't worry they will listen to you. But be patient because Pharaoh won't listen until he sees many signs and is punished, but after that he will let you go."

Moses still didn't think he was the right man for the job. "God what if the Israelites don't believe me, what if they say, 'I think you're lying, God didn't talk to you.'"

Then the Lord said to him, "Throw your staff on the ground." Moses did as he was told and his staff became a snake right before his eyes. Moses even jumped out of the way, the snake almost slithered right over his foot. Then the Lord said, "Pick it up by the tail." Moses didn't really like snakes but he quickly grabbed it by the tail and it turned from a limp yucky snake, to his smooth wooden staff right in his hand.

God continued to show Moses signs he could show the people so they would believe. Moses would even be able to turn water into blood because God would do it for him. Even after all these signs Moses still didn't think he could do it, and God was starting to get frustrated with his lack of trust. Moses would be able to do anything with God's help.

Finally God said to Moses, "I will send your brother Aaron, in fact he is already on his way to see you. I will help both of you, and give you the words to say." After that the bush stopped burning and God was gone.
So Moses put his sandals back on and made sure to take his staff of God, and went to get his wife and children to go to free the Israelites.

When Moses and his brother Aaron got to Egypt the Lord told them what to do. He said, "Go to Pharaoh and tell him to let the Israelites go. He will be very stubborn and it will take many signs and miracles before he will let you go; but everyone will know that I am God when he finally frees the Israelites."
The pharaoh refused to let the people go after all the plagues that happened because of his stubborness.

This day will always be known as the Passover, because you were passed over and kept safe by God. You will continue to celebrate this day for many years." Now you have to remember Pharaoh could have stopped all this a long time ago. God gave him many opportunities to let the Israelites go, but he would not listen. Unfortunately God had to teach Pharaoh a lesson and He did what He said He would do.

After Pharaoh realized what happened in Egypt he called for Moses and Aaron just after midnight and he said, "Leave my people, you and all the Israelites! Go worship the Lord as you wanted, take all your animals and get out of here!" The Israelites gathered up gold and silver from the Egyptians who were glad to see them leave and they left with Moses.

You won't believe what happened next! When Pharaoh heard that the Israelites had left he changed his mind- again! He decided to gather an army of more than 600 people and go after Moses, Aaron and all the Israelites.

So as the Israelites were on their way, they noticed in the distance that Pharaoh was coming after them. They started to get worried and questioned Moses why he would lead them out in the desert to die. Moses knew what to say, and he told them, "Do not be afraid, God has protected you before, He will protect you again."

When the Israelites reached the Red Sea they were trapped with the Sea in front of them and Pharaoh behind them. But God told Moses to reach out his staff into the water, and when he did an amazing thing happened. The water split into two! The water lifted itself and made huge walls of water (they couldn't even see over it, it was higher than a house). They would walk on dry ground, which was actually the bottom the Sea.

Pharaoh's army followed them into the Sea, even though some of the Egyptians were afraid, and knew God was with them. When the Israelites had finally made it through safe God told Moses, "Stretch out your hand over the sea so that the water goes back to normal, and it will swallow up Pharaoh and his army."

Moses did as God had told him and he reached his staff over the water. There was a loud crash as the water came back together, and covered the Egyptians.

That was the day the Lord saved the Israelites from the Egyptians. When the Israelites saw what God had done for them they trusted Him, and they knew that Moses would be a good leader for them as they traveled to the land flowing with milk and honey.

www.ingramcontent.com/pod-product-compliance
Lightning Source LLC
Chambersburg PA
CBHW081240130726
47997CB00009B/2939